The DG-14, built by Cameron Balloons, is the world's smallest ever helium-filled airship and can be stored in a normal hangar. She is 62 feet (19 metres) long, 27 feet (8 metres) high and has a capacity of 14,000 cubic feet (396 cubic metres).

AIRSHIPS

Patrick Abbott

Shire Publications Ltd

G000155796

CONTENTS

Copyright © 1991 by Patrick Abbott. First published 1991. Shire Album 259. ISBN 0 7478 0084 7.
All rights reserved. No part of this publication may be reproduced or transmitted in any form or by any means, electronic or mechanical, including photocopy, recording, or any information storage and retrieval system, without permission in writing from the publishers, Shire Publications Ltd, Cromwell House, Church Street, Princes Risborough, Buckinghamshire HP17 9AJ, UK.

Printed in Great Britain by C. I. Thomas & Sons (Haverfordwest) Ltd, Press Buildings, Merlins Bridge, Haverfordwest, Dyfed SA61 1XF.

British Library Cataloguing in Publication Data: Abbott, Patrick. Airships. 1. Airships, history. I. Title. 629. 1332409. ISBN 0-7478-0084-7.

ACKNOWLEDGEMENTS

Illustrations are acknowledged as follows: courtesy of the Advanced Airship Corporation, page 31; Aereon Corporation, page 29; Airship Industries, the cover and page 30 (top and bottom); Birmingham Post, page 28 (bottom left); Cameron Balloons, pages 1 and 28 (bottom right); Deutsches Museum, page 14 (above); Fleet Air Arm Museum, pages 4, 5 (above), 18 (top), 19 (top) and 21 (top); *Flight*, page 5 (below); Imperial War Museum, pages 12 (below), 13 (above), 14 (below), 18 (bottom), 19 (botttom), 20 (above), 21 (bottom), 22 (bottom), 25 (top) and 26 (top); Luftschiffbau Zeppelin, pages 13 (below) and 15; Musée de l'Air, pages 10 (inset) and 11; Museum of Flight, page 22 (top); Royal Aeronautical Society, pages 3, 24 (above left and below), 26 (bottom) and 28 (top); Science Museum, pages 7, 8 (above and below), 9 (above), 12 (above) 25 (bottom) and 27 (top); United Press International, page 27 (bottom).

Cover: *The third Skyship 500 (G-SKSA), which first flew in April 1983, flies over Manhattan. The advertising livery consists of banners that are fastened to the envelope and changed frequently.*

Below: *Schematic drawing of No 9, a typical rigid airship of 1917. Each of the seventeen compartments in the hull contained its own gasbag. This is a contemporary Admiralty drawing, with a slightly optimistic estimate of the top speed.*

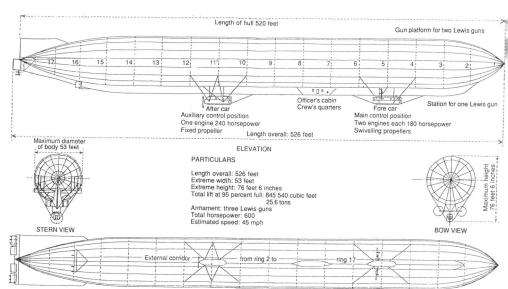

Length of hull 520 feet

Gun platform for two Lewis guns

Officer's cabin
Crew's quarters

After car
Auxiliary control position
One engine 240 horsepower
Fixed propeller

Length overall: 526 feet

Fore car
Main control position
Two engines each 180 horsepower
Swivelling propellers

Station for one Lewis gun

ELEVATION

Maximum diameter of body 53 feet

PARTICULARS

Length overall: 526 feet
Extreme width: 53 feet
Extreme height: 76 feet 6 inches
Total lift at 95 percent full: 845 540 cubic feet
25.6 tons
Armament: three Lewis guns
Total horsepower: 600
Estimated speed: 45 mph

Maximum height 76 feet 6 inches

STERN VIEW

BOW VIEW

External corridor from ring 2 to ring 17

VIEW FROM UNDERNEATH

SR1 was bought from the Italians and was the only semi-rigid ever employed by the Admiralty. She was 270 feet (82 metres) long and had a capacity of 441,000 cubic feet (12,500 cubic metres).

AIRSHIP PRINCIPLES

Flying machines that are propelled by engines but lifted by gasbags are termed dirigible balloons or airships. Such aircraft have nearly always used hydrogen, the lightest of all gases, as their lifting medium, but this possesses the disadvantages of being inflammable when pure and explosive when contaminated by air. If available, the much rarer gas helium is preferred, since, although it is less buoyant than hydrogen, it does not burn. Some small modern airships have used hot air instead of gas.

Lift depends on the weight of air which is displaced, less the weight of gas displacing it. Air weighs around 75 pounds (34 kg) for 1000 cubic feet (28 cubic metres), while a similar amount of hydrogen weighs only about 5 pounds (2 kg), so giving some 70 pounds (32 kg) of lift. The same volume of helium, by contrast, weighs about 10 pounds (4 kg) and so

gives 65 pounds (30 kg) of lift. In practical terms, each 32,000 cubic feet (907 cubic metres) of hydrogen contained by an airship will give about one ton of *gross lift*, but 34,500 cubic feet (977 cubic metres) of helium are needed for the same result.

From the gross lift is subtracted the weight of the airship's permanent structure to give the amount of *useful lift*, which can be allocated to the carrying of fuel, ballast, passengers and payload. But because gas expands or contracts according to temperature, altitude and other considerations — as does the surrounding atmosphere — the conditions of lift vary continually.

Unlike a free-floating balloon, an efficient airship cannot be spherical and slack but must be of a firm and streamlined form in order to cut its way through the air. To answer this essential require-

Lack of internal gas pressure can cause a non-rigid dirigible to lose its shape. The ballonets of this Coastal airship could not cope with the conditions.

ment, three types of dirigible were evolved: the non-rigid, the semi-rigid and the rigid. Airships of the first kind are still being built and flown today, but the other two types disappeared before the Second World War.

A non-rigid airship, often known as a *blimp*, is one consisting of a car or gondola fastened beneath a fabric envelope containing gas. In order to preserve the streamlining, the pressure within is carefully regulated by having smaller bags, called *ballonets*, incorporated inside the main gasbag. These are pumped with air or emptied as required, so maintaining the internal pressure of the envelope at the right level. The car carries both crew and engines, so when hydrogen was used, in order to avoid the risk of fire, it was always slung well below the envelope by rigging lines attached in some way to the outside. Airships using helium normally have the car fastened directly to the envelope, with rigging lines positioned internally.

A semi-rigid airship was normally larger than a non-rigid but had the same basic features, with the addition of a long internal keel running from bow to stern of the envelope to provide additional stiffening. This also allowed rigging lines to be placed inside the envelope, with cars attached directly to the keel.

As an airship — or any given shape — becomes larger, so the surface area increases as the square of the linear dimensions, while the volume increases as the cube. In other words, a large airship that is three times as long as a similarly shaped small airship has nine times as much surface area and drag, but 27 times as much volume and lift. It was to obtain the benefits of this inescapable mathematical rule that large rigid airships were evolved, for there are structural limits to the size a non-rigid can reach. Each rigid airship consisted of a huge streamlined framework of lightweight girders, covered by cloth and containing several drum-shaped balloons, each in its own compartment. However much gas was lost, or even if the gasbags were deflated completely, the rigid airship still retained its form intact. The girders were usually of duralumin, but wood was also used successfully.

An airship is controlled in flight by regulating the amount of lift; gas is released to descend and ballast — usually water — is released to ascend. Steering is by means of one or more vertical rudders attached to the tail fins and there are also horizontal rudders, termed *elevators*, which control the airship's attitude or *trim*. This can also be altered by moving the centres of gravity or lift in some manner, such as releasing ballast or gas at one extremity or shifting equipment. When flown in a nose-up attitude, an airship's envelope acts in the same

4

The hangar at Pulham, Norfolk, was more than 200 yards (183 metres) long. In July 1919 R33 and R34 were housed here side by side.

A rigid airship under construction. Three of the separate gasbags have already been inflated inside the framework of lightweight girders.

manner as an aeroplane's wing and gives *dynamic lift* which supplements the *static lift* of the gas. As this effect can also operate in reverse, it allows an airship to climb, dive or maintain height with the minimum loss of gas or ballast. Various lines are usually attached to the cars or to the envelope and these enable the ground crew to handle an airship safely in or out of its hangar.

All airships, of whatever type, have similar qualities. They are flimsy, because of their necessarily light construction, require large and expensive hangars when on the ground and are very slow.

No airship has yet reached a speed of even 100 mph (160 km/h). In compensation, they are economical, quiet and offer roomy accommodation; they can fly long distances without refuelling and are also much safer than the popular misconception. The great airship disasters of the past were caused by inadequate weather forecasting, bad design or the use of hydrogen. None of these considerations applies today and it is always forgotten that the only paying passengers ever to die in an airship accident were the thirteen who perished in the *Hindenburg*.

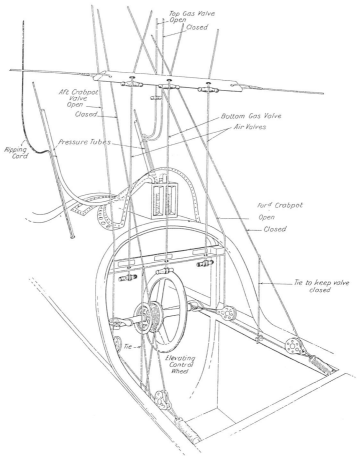

The cockpit of an SS airship, showing some of the controls.

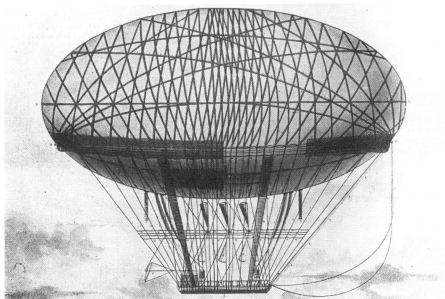

Meusnier's design of 1784. He anticipated many of the principles of the modern airship but knew of no suitable power source.

THE FIRST AIRSHIPS

The first projected lighter-than-air flying machine of all time was the strange vessel planned by an Italian, Francesco de Lana, in 1670, which was to have been propelled by sails and kept aloft by four hollow copper globes, from which the air had been exhausted to produce a vacuum. Although ingenious, the design was totally impracticable, for had it ever been built the globes would have simply collapsed under atmospheric pressure.

Another century passed before hot-air and gas balloons flew in 1783, but the first plans for a dirigible then followed almost immediately. Jean Meusnier, a French army officer, produced a design for a surprisingly sophisticated airship, which featured streamlining, rudder, propellers, rigging and even a ballonet. Unfortunately, no prototype was ever constructed, for the designer realised that no engine existed that was both light enough to be lifted by a gasbag and powerful enough to pull it through the air at a speed above a crawl. It was this factor which prevented real progress for more than a century afterwards.

The first airship upon which construction began was probably the *Dolphin* of 1816, designed by Pauly and Egg, two Swiss gunsmiths resident in London. This was the first to use a movable weight as a form of control, but it used oars in the car and strange flapping fins on each side of the envelope for propulsion. The project was abandoned, either because of public ridicule or through lack of funds.

It was not until 1852 that a partially successful airship was at last built. This was designed by a Frenchman, Henri Giffard, and had a cigar-shaped envelope without the safeguard of a ballonet. At a safe distance below the envelope hung a car containing a specially designed lightweight steam engine driving a large propeller. On 24th September 1852, carrying the inventor, the aircraft flew safely the 17 miles (27 km) from Paris to Trappes at a speed of around 6 mph (10 km/h),

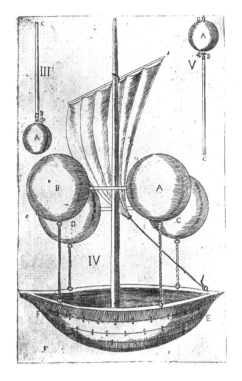

steering from side to side but unable to contend with the slight wind or to return to its starting place. Giffard later built a second and larger airship, but this time the lack of a ballonet caused it to buckle and crash. Failing eyesight prevented him from making further experiments, but his flight showed the world what would be possible once a lightweight power source could be found.

In an attempt to overcome this most intractable problem, two French brothers called Tissandier fitted an electric motor to the airship they constructed in 1882. During the next two years they made a few brief flights, but the results were disappointing and lack of funding prevented further experiments.

Nevertheless, their work was followed up by Renard and Krebs, two French army officers, who in 1884 designed and built a much more effective dirigible. Named *La France*, this was driven by a more powerful electric motor and used a

Left: *De Lana's projected airship of 1670. Despite its complete impracticability, it was the first design for a flying machine using the lighter-than-air principle.*

Below: *Durs Egg and John Pauly began building the 'Dolphin' at Knightsbridge in 1816. Known popularly as 'Egg's Folly', it was soon scrapped.*

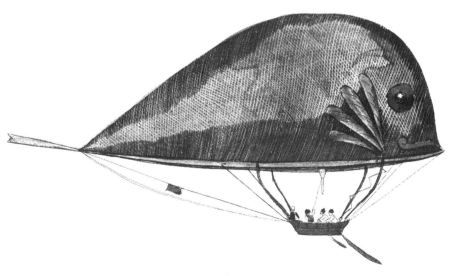

8

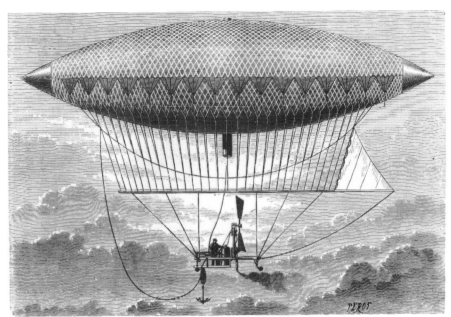

Henri Giffard's airship was unstable and underpowered. Nevertheless, it made what is usually regarded as the world's first dirigible flight in 1852.

The airship flown by the Tissandier brothers in 1883 used a cigar-shaped envelope similar to that of Giffard's dirigible.

Above, inset: *Alberto Santos Dumont, 1873-1932, the inventor and pilot of the world's first successful non-rigid airships.*

Right: *In 1901, to great popular acclaim, Santos Dumont flew round the Eiffel Tower in his sixth airship and won the Deutsch Prize.*

slim streamlined envelope provided with a ballonet, as well as an elevator plane and a sliding weight to control the trim. On 9th August 1884 *La France* lifted off from Chalais Meudon and flew nearly 5 miles (8 km) in 23 minutes, not only making progress against the wind, but completing a circle to land at its point of departure — a feat never before accomplished by any type of flying machine.

However, despite this initial success, the design proved impossible to develop further, as the weight of the batteries was too great for the airship to attain adequate speed or range.

But within the next few years the lightweight petrol engine, which was to make viable both the airship and the aeroplane, was developed. The first person to use the new power source with a dirigible —

or, indeed, with any type of aircraft — was Karl Wolfert, a German engineer, in 1897. Unhappily, his combined use of an open burner for the engine ignition and a car slung dangerously close to the envelope proved fatal; the airship crashed in flames during trials, killing the inventor and his passenger instantly.

Only a year later, a safer form of ignition became available and it was Alberto Santos Dumont, a Brazilian living in France, who finally brought together all the knowledge gained by his predecessors and built the world's first successful airships. His initial design flew in 1898 and, although slow and primitive, it was controllable and could make progress against a moderate wind. Improved versions soon followed and in 1901, with his sixth airship, Santos Dumont won the Deutsch Prize for the first flight from St Cloud, outside Paris, to the Eiffel Tower and back in less than half an hour. This was his most famous achievement, although in all he made fourteen airships and many outstanding flights, finally convincing the world that the age of flying had arrived. His No 9 was probably the smallest airship ever built

and flew regularly around Paris at rooftop height. In 1903 it was flown a short distance by a Cuban lady, Aida d'Acosta, who thus became the first and only woman ever to pilot an airship alone and unaccompanied.

The example of Santos Dumont encouraged experimenters throughout the world and soon non-rigid airships, all based on the same simple principles, were flying in many countries. The first airship flight in England was made by Stanley Spencer in 1902, but his craft was very underpowered, as was that of F. A. Barton in 1905. In September of the same year Ernest Willows made what was probably the first wholly successful dirigible flight in Britain and with a later model he became the first man to fly from England to France by airship. In 1907 the first British military airship, the *Nulli Secundus*, was built and, although too slow to be effective, it was followed by several other Army designs of increasing speed and efficiency. The most famous of these was *Beta*, a small non-rigid which became widely known to the public. She flew many hours in service and survived to carry out reconnaissance

Santos Dumont's No 9 was probably the smallest airship ever to be flown, with a capacity of only 7770 cubic feet (220 cubic metres).

11

'Nulli Secundus' was built at Farnborough by Colonel John Capper and Samuel Cody for the British Army. In October 1907 it was flown over central London before landing safely at the Crystal Palace.

The Army airship 'Beta' was 108 feet (33 metres) long, with a capacity of 42,000 cubic feet (1190 cubic metres).

Count Ferdinand von Zeppelin, 1838-1917, the inventor of the rigid airship.

and training work during the early months of the First World War.

While many nations made rapid advances in developing non-rigid dirigibles, France and Italy also experimented with semi-rigids and Germany concentrated on rigid airships. The man responsible for these huge and relatively sophisticated aircraft was Count Ferdinand von Zeppelin, whose name became inseparable from the airships themselves, although he was nearly 62 before the first of his aircraft — known as LZ1 — made a brief flight in September 1900. It was far bigger than the many small non-rigids soon to be flying elsewhere in the world and consisted of a cloth-covered aluminium framework, inside which were housed several separate gasbags, and below which were attached the engine cars. The dirigible was very slow and unimpressive, however, and although his second airship was much improved and showed promise it was soon wrecked by a storm when tethered in the open. His third, LZ3, first flew in October 1906

LZ3, the first successful rigid airship, made a flight of eight hours in 1907 and was subsequently bought by the German army.

and, despite still being rather slow, succeeded a year later in staying aloft for eight hours. In July 1908 the larger and more powerful LZ4 was completed and made a triumphant flight of more than twelve hours, when she reached a top speed of 40 mph (64 km/h), so proving the viability of the rigid airship beyond all doubt. Although this latest dirigible was also destroyed in a gale soon afterwards, Count Zeppelin had by now attracted sufficient support to finance the Zeppelin Foundation, which carried on the work of development. Within the next few years, several more rigid airships were built and the world's first commercial airline was established. During the four years preceding the First World War, these airships carried 10,197 passengers on 1588 flights and covered a total of 107,231 miles (172,567 km) without a single accident. But the zeppelins — as the airships themselves were now called — were also bought by the German army and navy, for it was their potential as weapons of war that ensured their fame in Germany and their notoriety in Britain.

The Zeppelin L32 was 649 feet (198 metres) long with a total gas capacity of 1,950,000 cubic feet (55,220 cubic metres) and a useful lift of nearly 30 tons. She was shot down in September 1916, with the loss of her entire crew.

This early SS airship was 143 feet (44 metres) long, with a diameter of 28 feet (8 metres) and a capacity of 60,000 cubic feet (1700 cubic metres). She carried a pilot and a radio operator, as well as a 250 pound (113 kg) bomb load and fuel for up to sixteen hours' cruising at half throttle. She had a top speed of around 50 mph (80 km/h) and could climb at 700 feet (213 metres) per minute.

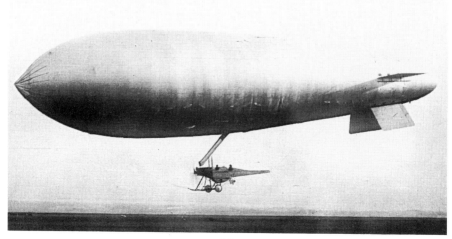

The L70 was one of the largest German wartime airships, being nearly 700 feet (213 metres) long and with a capacity of 2,200,000 cubic feet (62,300 cubic metres). She was the last zeppelin to be destroyed by British aircraft when she was shot down off the Norfolk coast on 5th August 1918 with the loss of all 22 of her crew.

THE FIRST WORLD WAR

During the First World War both Germany and Britain used airships in large numbers, but in very different ways and with very different results.

The German dirigibles were nearly all Zeppelin rigids: enormous and shapely aircraft, capable of fast rates of climb, great endurance and speeds equal to those of many contemporary aeroplanes. Around a hundred were built during the four years of war and they improved steadily in performance as the conflict continued. But although they sometimes acted as scouts for the German fleet, their potential for reconnaissance at sea was largely wasted. Instead of being used to seek out Allied convoys and to support

the U-boats, the German airships were sent to bomb Britain into submission, by raiding industry and terrifying the civilian population. It proved to be in vain, however, since although the zeppelins caused widespread panic the damage they inflicted on industry was relatively trivial, for their bomb loads were small and they flew only at night, when efficient navigation was difficult. Very soon, also, it became apparent that they were vulnerable to any form of incendiary bullet or shell, which ignited the hydrogen into a terrible conflagration that destroyed the airship within moments. British aeroplanes — becoming faster and better armed — were before long joining with

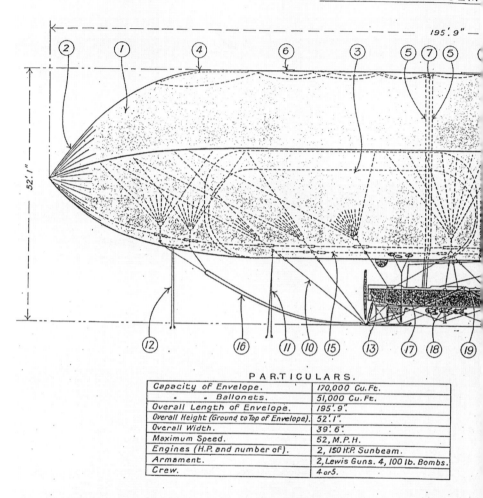

PARTICULARS.	
Capacity of Envelope.	170,000 Cu.Ft.
„ „ Ballonets.	51,000 Cu.Ft.
Overall Length of Envelope.	195'.9".
Overall Height (Ground to Top of Envelope).	52'.1".
Overall Width.	39'.6".
Maximum Speed.	52, M.P.H.
Engines (H.P. and number of).	2, 150 H.P. Sunbeam.
Armament.	2, Lewis Guns. 4, 100 lb. Bombs.
Crew.	4 or 5.

Schematic drawing of a Coastal type of airship, a typical non-rigid of 1917.

the anti-aircraft guns to wreak havoc on the invaders, many of which were shot down with the loss of all on board. In an attempt to avoid this ever present threat, the later German airships were made lighter and they flew at high altitudes in order to escape attack. This rendered their bombing even less effective and although occasional zeppelin raids con-

tinued until nearly the end of the war most of the later bombing was carried out by Gotha aeroplanes.

By contrast, Britain began the war with only seven small non-rigid airships, of which five were already obsolescent. There were no firm plans to build more until a few months later, when the German submarines began their attempt to

16

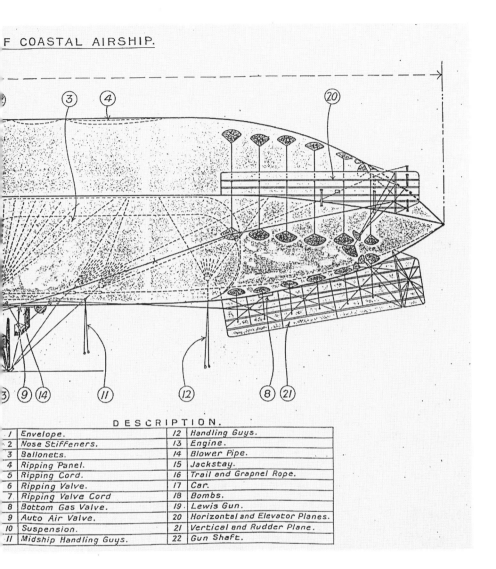

1	Envelope.	12	Handling Guys.
2	Nose Stiffeners.	13	Engine.
3	Ballonets.	14	Blower Pipe.
4	Ripping Panel.	15	Jackstay.
5	Ripping Cord.	16	Trail and Grapnel Rope.
6	Ripping Valve.	17	Car.
7	Ripping Valve Cord	18	Bombs.
8	Bottom Gas Valve.	19	Lewis Gun.
9	Auto Air Valve.	20	Horizontal and Elevator Planes.
10	Suspension.	21	Vertical and Rudder Plane.
11	Midship Handling Guys.	22	Gun Shaft.

starve Britain into defeat by the destruction of the shipping on which she depended for food and the raw materials of industry. The threat to Britain was extreme and protracted, so the Admiralty explored every means available to combat the U-boat menace. Not the least effective of these was the construction of more than two hundred airships to patrol the seas, escort convoys and watch for mines and submarines. Most of these airships were small, simple and rather primitive, but their deterrent value was excellent, for their observers were better placed than sailors to detect signs of U-boats and they could then attack them with bombs while calling by radio, semaphore or signal lamp to destroyers or

17

SS40 was the only airship to see active service with the British Army. In 1916 she was fitted with a larger envelope, painted black, to allow her to reach a height of up to 8000 feet (2438 metres) while operating at night over enemy lines.

armed merchantmen for help.

Although poorly armed for their own protection, the airships patrolled the seas around Britain with impunity, for U-boats could shoot at them only by surfacing, and as this made the submarines immediately vulnerable to armed shipping such retaliation was rarely attempted and never successful. At the same time the blimps were also safe from attack by German aeroplanes, since these did not usually have the range to reach them from the land. During the whole war enemy aeroplanes shot down only two British airships, both of which had strayed too close to German occupied territory.

The first British wartime airships were

C*1 was the first of the C Star Class, built in the last year of the war. She was 207 feet (63 metres) long and had a similar car to her predecessors but a more streamlined envelope with a capacity of 210,000 cubic feet (5950 cubic metres). In common with the other nine C Star airships, she survived the war without any major incident and was deleted in October 1919.

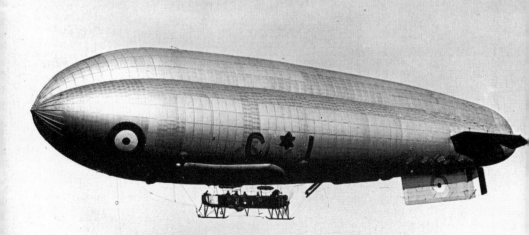

SSZ4 was one of the later Zero class of SS airships, with an enlarged envelope of 70,000 cubic feet (1982 cubic metres) capacity and a streamlined car carrying three crew members and a 75 horsepower Rolls-Royce engine. This was the most numerous class of British airships; 77 were built.

known as the Submarine Scout or SS class and were hastily built by fastening an aeroplane fuselage beneath a make-shift gasbag and adding radio, bombs and a larger petrol tank. These blimps cost only about £2500 each and, despite their crudity, they proved surprisingly effective. One, SS40, was even loaned to the Army for night-time reconnaissance on the Western Front and so became the only British airship ever to fly over enemy territory. Later versions became larger, faster and better equipped, although most of them were still handicapped by having only one engine, at a time when these were very unreliable. Several

The car of SSZ27 showing the high mounting of the engine, which enabled the airship to alight and take off from the sea. A Lewis gun was provided for defence and this could be mounted on either side of the forward cockpit.

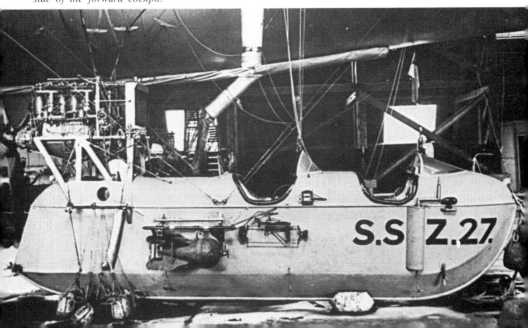

Airships worked in partnership with destroyers and other armed vessels. Here SSZ37 is flying over the PC61, a patrol boat built to resemble a merchant ship. Both were based at Pembroke.

C20 was a Coastal airship stationed at East Fortune in East Lothian, Scotland. She was 195 feet (59 metres) long, with a capacity of 170,000 cubic feet (4814 cubic metres) and carried a bomb load of 448 pounds (203 kg), together with one Lewis machine-gun in the car and another on top of the envelope. She was lost at sea in December 1917. 35 Coastal class airships were built altogether.

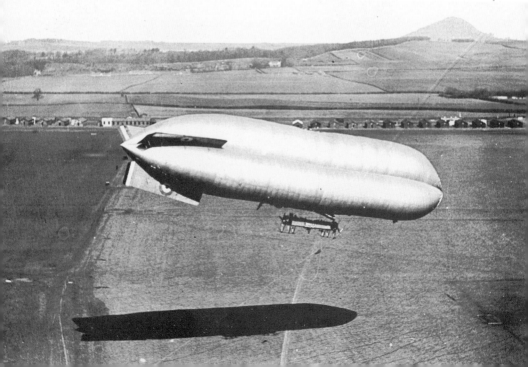

No 9 was the first British rigid to fly. She was 526 feet (160 metres) long and 53 feet (16 metres) in diameter, with a total gas capacity of 846,000 cubic feet (23,959 cubic metres). Modelled on earlier German designs, she was much too heavy for efficiency and even after substantial modifications she had a top speed of only 43 mph (69 km/h) and a useful lift of only 3.8 tons, including a bomb load of only 300 pounds (136 kg).

of the SS airships flew a total of more than one thousand hours on active service.

Other larger types of airship were also developed to provide increased range and efficiency. The most successful were probably the blimps of the Coastal class, which had cars made from two aeroplane fuselages cut short and fastened together end to end. They had envelopes of a trilobe shape, were powered by two engines mounted in tandem and usually carried a crew of five. The most famous of these was C9, which flew a record 2500 hours in service and attacked several submarines during an outstanding career. The Coastal class was followed by the C Star class, which were modified and improved versions of the Coastal, and by the North Sea class, which were powered

by two engines mounted side by side and were the largest non-rigids designed in Britain during the war. Despite early problems they eventually proved to be very efficient, as they were fitted with enclosed cabins, sleeping accommodation and cooking facilities, so enabling them to carry two crews and to patrol for long periods without returning to base. Flights of more than 24 hours were commonplace and one airship, NS11, put up a world record in February 1919 when she stayed up for 100 hours 50 minutes.

Only towards the end of the war were rigid airships acquired by the Admiralty, and these were mostly rather inferior copies of early German Zeppelin designs, slightly altered. The first of them was No 9, which proved to be much too heavy and slow even after considerable and

NS4 was one of fourteen airships of the North Sea class. She was 260 feet (80 metres) long, with a diameter of 57 feet (17 metres) and a capacity of 360,000 cubic feet (10,200 cubic metres). She was powered by two 240 horsepower Fiat engines and had a useful lift of 3.8 tons, which usually included three Lewis guns and a bomb load of 12 cwt (610 kg).

R29 was basically the same design as No 23, but with the keel removed. This modification made her much lighter and enabled her to turn more quickly. Like her sister ship R27, she had a useful lift of 8.5 tons. These were the only two airships of the 23X class to be built.

drastic modification. She finally entered service in April 1917 but carried out only one patrol before being relegated to training and experimental duties. She was followed by four slightly larger airships of the No 23 class, which proved to be only a little better, and two of the 23X class, which were rather more effective. There was also R31, a wooden-framed airship which was commissioned less than a week before the Armistice but eventually fell to pieces when abandoned for many months in a damp and damaged hangar.

Of the eight rigids which saw service during the war, No 9 was declared obsolete and deleted before the Armistice, as was R27, which was destroyed in a hangar fire. The other six survived some months longer but despite their expense — each one cost some £125,000 — none proved very successful. Their total flying time was very small and they contributed little towards the war effort, being employed only occasionally on patrols or convoy duties. No 23 and R26 both made publicity flights over wartime London, to boost civilian morale, but the only British rigid airship to see action was R29, which joined with destroyers to sink a submarine in September 1918.

No 23 was basically an improvement to the No 9 design, with another bay inserted and further lightening. She was 535 feet (163 metres) long and had a capacity of 942,000 cubic feet (26,677 cubic metres) and a useful lift of 6.5 tons. Powered by four 250 horsepower Rolls-Royce engines, she had a top speed of 52 mph (84 km/h). Four ships of this class were built.

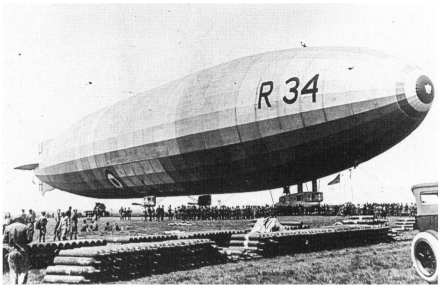

R34 was 643 feet (196 metres) long, with a total capacity of 1,950,000 cubic feet (55,224 cubic metres). She was powered by five 250 horsepower Sunbeam engines and had a top speed of only 54 mph (87 km/h). She was destroyed at her moorings by a gale in 1921.

BETWEEN THE WARS

After the First World War Britain scrapped her fleet of non-rigid airships almost immediately, and, although rigids continued in limited use for a short while, only six more were completed and only one of these proved to be wholly successful. This was R34, copied from the design of a wrecked zeppelin and commissioned in early 1919. In July of that year, only weeks after Alcock and Brown had made the first non-stop crossing of the Atlantic by air, she flew from East Fortune in Scotland to New York in 108 hours 12 minutes, which was a world endurance record, beating that set up by NS11 a few months earlier. She returned to Pulham in Norfolk in 75 hours 3 minutes, having accomplished the first east to west flight of the Atlantic, the first double crossing and the first crossing by an airship. She was also the first aircraft to fly directly either way between the United Kingdom and the United States. Not for more than a decade was an aeroplane able to repeat this feat.

Two years later, R38 was completed, for sale to the United States. She was based on German practice, but by British designers with little experience of reconciling the twin demands of strength and lightness. On 24th August 1921, when on a trial flight, she was turned too tightly and broke in two, falling into the Humber. Of the 49 men on board only five survived. Her loss brought an end to the use of military dirigibles in Britain and the surviving rigid airships were grounded and eventually scrapped. Later in the decade, however, a final attempt to produce civilian airships for passenger flight was made.

Two large rigid airships were ordered, in virtual competition with each other, one to be privately funded and one to be built with government money. The former was R100, which was undoubtedly the best airship ever made in Britain, and the latter was R101, which was possibly the worst. Both flew for the first time in late 1929 and R100 soon proved

Left: *Air-Commodore Edward Maitland, CMG, DSO, AFC, 1880-1921, was the senior officer of Britain's Airship Service. He crossed the Atlantic in R34 and died in the R38 disaster.*

Right: *Major G. H. Scott, CBE, AFC, 1888-1930, was captain of No 9 and R34. He was killed in the R101 disaster.*

Below: *R34 descending at New York in July 1919, after four and a half days in the air.*

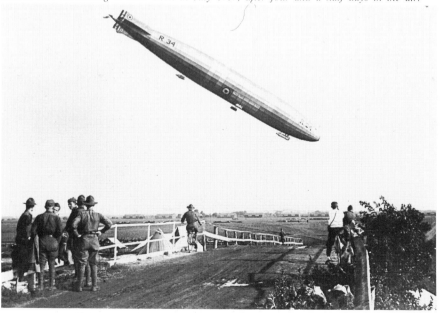

R101 was the largest ever British airship. Her original length of 732 feet (223 metres) was extended to 777 feet (237 metres) by the insertion of an extra bay, when her total capacity became 5,500,000 cubic feet (155,760 cubic metres).

to be both fast and reliable. During the following July and August she made a two-way crossing of the Atlantic to Canada and back with little trouble and seemed set for a secure future. R101, in contrast, was beset by problems which her designers were given insufficient time to rectify. Eventually, despite the misgivings of her crew, she left Cardington, Bedfordshire, on her way to India, only to crash into a hillside near Beauvais, France, in the early hours of 5th October 1930. She caught fire instantly, 48 of the 54 people on board being burnt to death. This tragedy ended all British involvement in airships; R100 was immediately scrapped and another generation passed before a British dirigible again took to the air.

The Italians had meanwhile concentrated on developing the semi-rigid type of airship. The most famous of these was *Norge*, in which the Norwegian explorer

Amundsen flew from Spitzbergen over the North Pole to Alaska in 1926, covering a total distance of around 3000 miles (4800 km). A second expedition two years later was led by Umberto Nobile and used a sister ship, *Italia*, but she crashed into the ice far from base. Many lives were lost before the survivors were rescued.

The Americans alone possessed adequate supplies of the safe gas helium, and this encouraged them to persevere with airships of all sizes. Their small blimps were notably efficient, but the three rigids which were also built proved to be uniformly unlucky and were all destroyed by storms. The *Shenandoah* broke in two over Ohio in September 1925, when 29 survived out of her crew of 43. In 1933 the *Akron* was forced down into the sea and only three of her 77 crew survived in what remains the world's worst ever airship disaster. Two

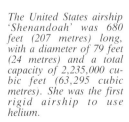

The United States airship 'Shenandoah' was 680 feet (207 metres) long, with a diameter of 79 feet (24 metres) and a total capacity of 2,235,000 cubic feet (63,295 cubic metres). She was the first rigid airship to use helium.

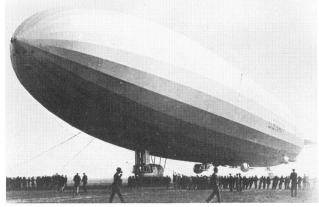

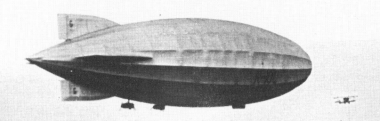

R100 was 709 feet (216 metres) long, with a diameter of 130 feet (40 metres) and a capacity of 5,000,000 cubic feet (141,600 cubic metres).

years later her sister ship, *Macon*, crashed in a very similar accident, but all but two of her 83 crew were rescued. After this latest tragedy, the United States abandoned the development of rigid airships entirely, although the small blimps continued to be used by the US Navy for many years.

Appropriately, however, it was from Germany that there came the most famous airship of all time. Immediately after the First World War the Zeppelin Company had built two civilian airships, but these had been confiscated by the Allies, together with the last of the wartime airships. The next one to be produced, the *Los Angeles*, was flown to the United States as part of the war reparations and it was not until 1928 that the first flight took place of the airship that was to prove the greatest of all dirigibles.

She was the *Graf Zeppelin* and for more than a decade she flew as no other airship has ever flown, with safety, comfort and reliability. She crossed the Atlantic more than a hundred times, flew more than a million miles altogether, became the only airship to circumnavigate the world and never lost a life. So successful was she that despite the refusal of the United States to provide helium an even bigger airship was built, to provide regular transatlantic passenger services. This was the *Hindenburg*, the largest flying machine ever made, and after successful trials she made her first commercial flight to America in 1937, arriving at the New Jersey airport on the evening of 6th May. When only seconds away from an uneventful landing and for reasons that have never been satisfactorily explained, she exploded into flames and was totally

The 'Hindenburg' was the largest aircraft of all time: 803 feet (245 metres) long, 135 feet (41 metres) in diameter and with a capacity of 7,000,000 cubic feet (198,240 cubic metres).

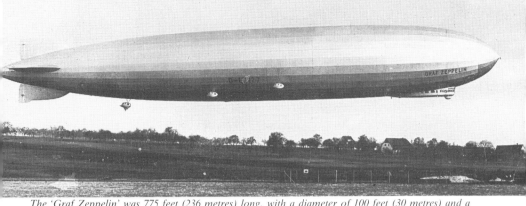

The 'Graf Zeppelin' was 775 feet (236 metres) long, with a diameter of 100 feet (30 metres) and a total gas capacity of 3,700,000 cubic feet (104,784 cubic metres). Her top speed was 80 mph (129 km/h) with a cruising speed of 68 mph (109 km/h).

destroyed. Of the 97 people on board at the time, 62 came out alive, while 22 crew members and thirteen passengers perished. A sister ship was constructed and flew briefly before the outbreak of war, but in 1940 both she and the *Graf Zeppelin* were broken up for the scrap value of their metal frameworks. They remain to this day the last rigid airships to have flown.

The destruction of the 'Hindenburg' on 6th May 1937 in New Jersey.

The four ships of the ZPG-3W class were the largest non-rigids ever made, with a capacity of 1,500,000 cubic feet (42,480 cubic metres) and a length of 403 feet (123 metres).

AIRSHIPS TODAY

The United States was the only nation to persevere with the use of small non-rigid airships and their naval blimps were deployed very effectively throughout the Second World War. Afterwards, their use continued and for several years they patrolled with radar scanners rotating inside the helium of their envelopes. The last and most sophisticated of these airships were the four blimps of the ZPG-3W class, the largest and fastest non-rigids ever built. Together with others, they provided an essential part of the early warning system, until improvements in radar technology rendered them no longer necessary. In 1964 the last Airship Group of the United States Navy was disbanded although the Goodyear Company, which had built the navy's airships, continued to maintain a small fleet of blimps for publicity and advertising purposes. One of these was for some

Left: The Goodyear blimp 'Europa' flying over Birmingham in 1972. She was used primarily for advertisement purposes.

Right: The DP-90 is a hot-air dirigible built to order by Cameron Balloons of Bristol. She has a total capacity of 90,000 cubic feet (2550 cubic metres) and can carry two persons.

Right and below right: The Aereon aircraft has yet to be built. She is planned to be part airship and part aeroplane, possibly 1000 feet (305 metres) long and capable of carrying up to 1000 tons of cargo by dynamic lift.

years based in Europe and appropriately named *Europa*. She was a small and conventional craft, differing little from her predecessors.

Despite the demise of the military blimp, there is renewed interest in the use of civilian airships, possibly for the carrying of cargo. The airship, unlike any other type of transport, is potentially capable of collecting goods from a factory and delivering them directly and economically to a retailer anywhere in the world, cutting out all the intermediate stages of lorries, docks, shipping, docks and lorries again. Several projects for building such a cargo airship have appeared, among them the extraordinary Aereon machines, which combine the characteristics of both the airship and the aeroplane. None has yet been built, however, since the investment needed would be enormous.

Nevertheless, orthodox airship development has recommenced and Britain leads the world in the new technologies involved. The company mainly concerned is Airship Industries and, al-

though its dirigibles are basically little different in principle from their First World War predecessors, they are vastly superior in detailed design and benefit from the use of new materials and the ready availability of helium. Two basic types of dirigible are produced: the Skyship 500 and the slightly larger Skyship 600. In each, the car is a monocoque structure, built from reinforced plastic, and attached directly to the lower side of the envelope, but supported internally by rigging lines reaching up to the top. Two ballonets are fitted and they are fed by air collected from the slipstreams of the two propellers, mounted on either side of the car. These can be swivelled to provide vectored thrust, so pushing the airship upwards or downwards. The envelope material is laminated, lined with a gas-retention film and sprayed externally with a polyurethane coating. In flight the airships are stable, manoeuvrable, comfortable and safe. They are used for advertising, tourist flights, fishery patrols and a variety of other duties.

Between 1979 and 1989 Airship Indus-

A Skyship 500 built by Airship Industries in 1981. She is 171 feet (52 metres) long, with a diameter of 46 feet (14 metres) and a capacity of 182,000 cubic feet (5,154 cubic metres).

tries built fifteen airships, of which six have been sold to other operators. Two much larger dirigibles are being designed, one of which — to be known as the *Sentinel 5000* — has been ordered by the United States Navy as an AEW (Airborne Early Warning) airship. When completed, it will be the largest non-rigid ever made. After that, a civilian variant may be built, to be known as the

A Skyship 600 airship, built in 1984. She is 194 feet (59 metres) long, with a diameter of 50 feet (15 metres) and a capacity of 235,400 cubic feet (6,666 cubic metres).

The ANR airship will be 200 feet (60.96 metres) long, 50 feet (15.24 metres) in diameter and have a capacity of 256,724 cubic feet (7,270 cubic metres). A photograph of a model.

Skyship 5000. Such an aircraft would carry more passengers than the *Hindenburg*, travel faster than the *Queen Mary*, provide more comfort than a Boeing 747 and be safer than all three.

Another British firm, Thunder and Colt of Oswestry in Shropshire, produces small helium airships for the commercial market as well as a range of dirigibles using hot air for lift. The largest of these — built to special order for the purpose of surveying the Brazilian rain forests — is the AS 261. This is the world's largest ever hot-air airship and it can carry a crew of five as well as a payload of nearly one ton.

At the other extreme, Cameron Balloons of Bristol, Europe's largest manufacturer of balloons, builds and sells very small hot-air airships. The company also produces the world's smallest ever helium airship, the DG-14, which is simple to house, maintain and fly, and relatively inexpensive.

Yet another British company, the Advanced Airship Corporation of Jurby, Isle of Man, is preparing the prototype of a new passenger airship to be known as the ANR (Advanced Non Rigid). This is intended for a wide variety of roles and at moderate speeds will be capable of remaining airborne for more than three days. Alternatively, it will be able to reach a speed of more than 90 mph (145 km/h) and carry up to thirty passengers.

The peculiar advantages of the airship are at last becoming widely recognised and after a generation of neglect they are returning to the skies.

FURTHER READING

Abbott, Patrick. *Airship — The Story of R34*. Adams and Dart, 1973.
Abbott, Patrick. *The British Airship at War*. Terence Dalton, 1989.
Chamberlain, G. *Airships Cardington*. Terence Dalton, 1984.
Clarke, Basil. *The History of Airships*. Herbert Jenkins, 1961.
Guttery, T. E. *Zeppelin: An Illustrated Life of Count Ferdinand von Zeppelin, 1838-1917*. Shire Publications, 1973.
Higham, Robin. *The British Rigid Airship*. G. T. Foulis, 1961.
Jackson, Robert. *Airships*. Cassell, 1971.
Kinsey, G. *Pulham Pigs*. Terence Dalton, 1988.
Meager, George. *My Airship Flights*. William Kimber, 1970.
Poolman, Kenneth. *Zeppelins over England*. Evans Brothers, 1960.
Raleigh, W., and Jones, A. H. *The War in the Air*. Clarendon, 1969.
Robinson, Douglas. *Giants in the Sky*. G. T. Foulis, 1971.
Robinson, Douglas. *The Zeppelin in Combat*. G. T. Foulis, 1966.
Toland, John. *Ships in the Sky*. Frederick Muller, 1957.
Vaeth, J. G. *Graf Zeppelin*. Frederick Muller, 1959.
Ventry, Lord, and Kolesnik, E. M. *Airship Saga*. Blandford, 1982.
Williams, T. B. *Airship Pilot No. 28*. William Kimber, 1974.

PLACES TO VISIT

Intending visitors are advised to find out the opening times before making a special journey.

GREAT BRITAIN
Fleet Air Arm Museum, Royal Naval Air Station, Yeovilton, Yeovil, Somerset BA22 8AT. Telephone: 0935 840565. Models of No 9 and Coastal airship. Memorabilia.
Museum of Army Flying, Middle Wallop, Stockbridge, Hampshire SO20 8DY. Telephone: 0264 62121 extensions 4421 and 4428. Engine of *Nulli Secundus*.
Museum of Flight, East Fortune Airfield, North Berwick, East Lothian EH39 5LF. Telephone: 062088 308. Model and memorabilia of R34. Models of British wartime airships.
Royal Air Force Museum, Grahame Park Way, Hendon, London NW9 5LL. Telephone: 081-205 2266. Car of R33. Memorabilia.
Science Museum, Exhibition Road, South Kensington, London SW7 2DD. Telephone: 071-938 8000. Large number of models of all types of airship. Car of *Beta*. Memorabilia. Engines.

FRANCE
Musée de l'Air et de l'Espace, Aeroport du Bourget, 93350 Le Bourget, Paris. Models and memorabilia.

GERMANY
Städtisches Bodensee Museum, Adenauer Platz 1, 7990 Friedrichshafen, Baden-Württemberg. Models of Zeppelin airships and memorabilia.

UNITED STATES OF AMERICA
National Air and Space Museum, Seventh Street and Independence Avenue, SW, Washington DC 20560. Models and memorabilia.